Cover to Cover
Bible Study

7 Sessions for Homegroup
and Personal Use

C000242054

The Prodigal Son

Amazing grace

Rob Frost

CWR

Published 2006 by CWR, Waverley Abbey House, Waverley Lane, Farnham, Surrey GU9 8EP, UK. Registered Charity No. 294387. Registered Limited Company No. 1990308. Reprinted 2008, 2010.

See back of book for list of National Distributors.

Unless otherwise indicated, all Scripture references are from the Holy Bible: New International Version (NIV), copyright © 1973, 1978, 1984 by the International Bible Society.

Concept development, editing, design and production by CWR
Cover photograph: Dan Morrice and Chris Raven
Printed in Latvia by Yeomans Press Ltd

ISBN: 978-1-85345-412-7

Contents

Introduction

We often sing the hymn 'Amazing grace', and most of us have an idea that it has something to do with God's love for us.

The story of John Newton, the writer of that popular hymn, is a remarkable illustration of what God's grace can do in a person's life. He moved from being a slave trader to one of the key opponents to the slave trade. His story shows that when God's grace touches one life, it can have a wonderful effect on the lives of many others.

Grace is a far more rich and complex gift than most of us recognise. And our Christian lives would be all the richer and more meaningful if we could really grasp something of its profundity.

Each of these seven studies explores a different aspect of grace, and even when we've covered these seven ... there will still be more to comprehend! Such is the 'amazing' quality of God's grace.

Scholars warn against pushing the message of Jesus' parable of the prodigal son 'too far'. A parable is a story which allows listeners to 'draw their own conclusions', and that is how Jesus intended it to be used. In making seven studies out of this one story I may have allegorised it more than I should and applied the 'father figure' to our understanding of God too frequently. Where possible, however, I have attempted to encourage the group members to 'draw their own conclusions' about each part of the story and tried to keep in tune with its parabolic nature.

Scholars tell us that this is a story about a man who lost two sons, one to a life of reckless living and the other to a life of religious pride. Above all it is a hard-hitting challenge to the religious Jews to discover the meaning God's grace.

In the first study, 'The Hard Goodbye', we'll begin to understand how God's gift of 'free will' is a mark of His great love for us.

In the second study, 'In the Pigsty', we discover that – even in the filth and stench of our sinfulness and rebellion – we can still smell the fragrance of a love which reaches out to us right where we are. Grace reaching out to us, even when we live as though God doesn't care!

In the third study, 'The Long Road Home', we discover how grace is active in calling us to repentance and in enabling us to take the first step towards 'saying sorry' and starting again.

In the fourth study, 'A Robe and a Ring', we discover that, even in the self-condemnation which the son feels, God's love reaches out to him, receives him and forgives him … even when he can't forgive himself. This is the grace of the new beginning!

In the fifth study, 'Dead and Alive', we discover something of the beautiful relationship which the father wants to share with his son. The son is not welcomed back as a 'hired hand', but as a member of the family who shares a new and even richer relationship with his father. This is indeed abundant grace!

In the sixth study, 'Party Time', we learn how we should celebrate grace, and how Christians need to enter into the joy of the woman who found the coin, the shepherd who found his sheep and the father who found his son. We need to learn how to 'party' when grace is around!

In the final study, 'Sour Grapes', we are alerted to ways in which we can live without an appreciation of grace in our lives. We learn from the older son that, in judging others, we can lose the favour of God. If we are too religious or proud ... we can miss the very core of what the Christian message is all about!

The success of this series of studies depends on the willingness of the members of the group to share deeply with each other. There are lots of opportunities for people to wrestle with big questions and to apply this teaching to their lives.

My hope is that these studies will be far more than a biblical exploration of grace! My hope is that we may all live in a fuller awareness of the 'amazing grace of Jesus' day by day.

WEEK 1

The Hard Goodbye

Opening Icebreaker

Describe some of the happy and sad 'goodbyes' that you have known in your life. Is the way that we say 'goodbye' important?

Get Involved ...

Imagine the prodigal son at a bar with one of his mates. He's saying goodbye to him, and telling him what it was like for him to say goodbye to his dad!

Bible Reading

The Prodigal Son: Luke 15:11–20

Dig Deeper

1. Why do you think that the son wanted the money so soon?
2. Why was the father so willing to give him his inheritance early?
3. What do you think the son would have done if the father had refused?
4. How do you think that the son felt as he took the money?
5. How do you think that the father felt as he handed over the money?
6. What did the son's departure do to the father and how do you think it affected their relationship?
7. What would you have said to the son as he prepared to leave?
8. What would you have said to the father after the door banged shut?
9. What do you think that the father wished most for his son?
10. What do you think the son wished for his own life?

Insight Readings

Our three insight readings all explore the stories of people who set out on a journey away from God ... a similar journey to the prodigal son's.

In small groups read one of the passages, and try to 'get into' the thinking of the main characters.

Adam and Eve: Genesis 3:1–13
Why do you think that Adam and Eve chose to 'eat of the tree' rather than to obey God's will?

The rich young ruler: Matthew 19:16–22
Why did the rich young ruler choose to walk away rather

than 'give away all his money to the poor'?

Judas Iscariot: Matthew 26:20–25
Why did Judas choose to betray Jesus rather than to stand
with him?

Insight Comment

We often read in the Bible of situations in which God's
people go their own way, and of stories in which He
even allows them to run headlong into a life of rebellion
and self-destruction.

In the Garden of Eden, God could have ring-fenced the
Tree of Life with a 100-foot-high electric wire, but instead
He simply asked Adam and Eve not to eat of its fruit. He
gave them free will – the right to choose, to rebel and
to go their own selfish way. It's little wonder, then, that
when God walked in the garden they felt so ashamed,
and wanted to hide!

This kind of generous offer to choose, with no strings
attached, is the hallmark of genuine love. It is one of
the ways by which we know just how much God loves
us. He makes no attempt to control our will; He just sets
us free to make our own choices and to make our own
mistakes.

When Jesus met the rich young ruler and offered him
salvation, the cost involved in saying 'yes' to Jesus was
too great for him to accept. The call to follow Jesus
involves selflessness and sacrifice. It was too great a price
for him to pay. But Jesus did not run after him, try to
make him change his mind or beg him to think again. He
simply let him go! Jesus must have been heartbroken at
the choice which the rich young ruler made … but He
didn't stop him.

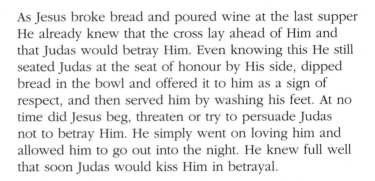

As Jesus broke bread and poured wine at the last supper He already knew that the cross lay ahead of Him and that Judas would betray Him. Even knowing this He still seated Judas at the seat of honour by His side, dipped bread in the bowl and offered it to him as a sign of respect, and then served him by washing his feet. At no time did Jesus beg, threaten or try to persuade Judas not to betray Him. He simply went on loving him and allowed him to go out into the night. He knew full well that soon Judas would kiss Him in betrayal.

At various times during our lifetime we will arrive at a kind of crossroads where we will have to make a straight choice. The choice which faces us may be as stark as choosing to do God's will or to reject it. To go God's way, or to go our own.

The amazing thing about grace is that we are given this kind of choice at all. God did not create us to be remote-controlled robots or mindless automatons. He gave us a mind and a heart and He took the risk of giving us free will.

This freedom to choose is a mark of His love for us. The hallmark of grace is that He does not control us, but liberates us to make our own decisions and even to make our own mistakes.

God's grace says, 'You are free to choose your own path and to make your own mistakes. You are even free to reject Me and to turn your back on My love.'

The starting point for our understanding of grace, then, is to comprehend just how costly this gift is. In giving us 'free will' God trusts us. He reaches out to us and says, 'I love you so much that I will even give you the right to reject Me and to go your own way.' And that really is amazing grace!

Discussion Starters

1. Why didn't Jesus chase after the rich young ruler, or follow Judas into the night to ask him to 'think again'?

2. Why was Adam hiding in the Garden of Eden when God was walking there? How do we hide from God … and why?

3. Why did God give us 'free will'? Wouldn't it have been a lot easier if He'd kept control of us?

4. What would life be like if we didn't have 'free will'? Is 'free will' a mixed blessing?

5. What kind of struggles do we face in going 'God's way' rather than our own? Try to describe some of those situations which you have faced in your own life.

Open Our Eyes

I once had a very traumatic experience under the sea. It happened during my first, and as it turned out, my last, attempt at scuba diving. I was given a few minutes of instruction by a diver on a Spanish beach and told that I must swim underwater beside him. Under no circumstances was I to come to the surface without him by my side.

This was all very well until he swam at such speed that gradually his flippers disappeared in a cloud of bubbles ahead of me and I was left there under the sea, feeling all alone! Remembering his stern instruction that I must not surface, I descended a couple more metres to the ocean floor and stood there, wondering what to do ... and waiting. I was there for some considerable time.

I learned later that my instructor had gone to the surface, hailed the diving launch and proceeded to circle the bay looking for my bubbles! That wait on the ocean floor was one of the longest waits of my life. But right there, deep below the surface of the sea, with fish swimming all around me, a verse from the Bible popped into my head and I found myself repeating it to myself over and over again.

> Where can I go from your Spirit? Where can I flee from your presence? If I go up to the heavens, you are there; if I make my bed in the depths, you are there. (Psa. 139:7–8)

I had discovered that even there, alone, desperate and close to the 'world of the dead', He was with me.

This is what God's grace is like. Even if we hide on the highest mountaintop or in the deepest ocean ... He will still find us ... and still love us. Grace reaches out to us ... even in our disobedience.

WEEK 2

In the Pigsty

Opening Icebreaker

Describe some of the jobs you've done in your life.

- What was your worst job?

- How did it feel when you were doing it?

- How did others treat you?

- What did you most want to happen when you were doing this job?

Get Involved ...

Discuss what life on a pig farm might have been like at the time of this story. What would the working day have consisted of, what kind of people would have worked there, and how would it have felt? How hungry must you be to fancy a bowl of pig-swill?

Bible Reading
The Prodigal Son: Luke 15:13–17

Dig Deeper

1. Why do you think the son went to a 'distant country'?
2. How do you think he managed to spend so much, so quickly?
3. How must it have felt to have gone from such plenty to such poverty?
4. Why did the people who had been with him desert him so quickly?
5. How would the listeners have felt when Jesus told them that the prodigal was feeding pigs?
6. 'But no one gave him anything.' Why?

The amazing thing about God's grace is that it is much stronger and more resilient than many of us recognise! Although the son had rejected his father, squandered his inheritance and ended up in a pigsty the father still loved him. Even when we run away from God His grace is still present ... and still at work in our situation.

Insight Readings

Our three 'insight' readings all explore the stories of people who discovered that God was still with them ...

even in their disobedience.

In small groups read one of the passages, and try to 'get into' the thinking of the main characters.

Jonah 1 (focus on v.17)
Why was the 'big fish' a sign of God's grace?

Nehemiah 1 (focus on vv.8–9)
What does this passage tell us about God's grace?

John 20 (focus on v.25)
In this important exchange between Jesus and Thomas, what do we learn about grace ... even in doubt?

Insight Comment

There is a resilience about God's grace which many of us underestimate. We often measure the love of God by human standards, but human love can be fickle, it can easily take offence and walk away.

In our three insight passages we see how God's grace still remains active even in our disbelief and disobedience.

Jonah had rejected God's call to Nineveh and in complete disobedience had set sail to Tarshish. When he was floundering around in the ocean God's grace provided a 'way of escape' through the 'big fish'. It was a time for repentance, a new start, and a new opportunity for Jonah to return to God's plan for his life.

Time and again the people of Israel muttered against their leaders, rejected God's way and ambled around the wilderness in a state of complete disobedience! Yet time and again, as we see in Nehemiah 1:9, God makes them a generous offer: 'If you return to me ...'

The grace of Jesus is illustrated in his relationship with Thomas. Thomas has the evidence of close friends and witnesses, but he remains in disbelief until he sees the risen Lord for himself. Even here, in his disobedience of saying 'I will not believe it' Jesus reaches out to him. God's grace is tough, durable and hard-wearing. Even when we have done our best to destroy it, to run away from it and to reject it … it is still there. God simply goes on loving us, waiting for us and reaching out to us.

The way of the world is to 'name and shame' those who have 'fallen from grace'. The tabloids tell their lurid stories and spell out the pornographic details of their moral failure.

God does not take pleasure in the situation of those who have ended up 'in the pigsty'. Yet God's aim is not to destroy or to humiliate but to hope the best for us. But His grace doesn't do all the work. It demands a response from us, a change in our world-view and a new kind of lifestyle. All this comes as a response to the grace of God at work within us.

In his classic devotional guide *My Utmost for His Highest* Oswald Chambers wrote:

> We cannot do what God does, and God will not do what we can do. We cannot save ourselves nor sanctify ourselves, God does that; but God will not give us good habits, He will not give us character, He will not make us walk aright. We have to do all that ourselves, we have to work out the salvation God has worked in.

Discussion Starters

1. Do you believe that God ever washes His hands of people, and stops caring about what happens to them

2. When people deliberately turn away from God, reject His laws and discard His plans ... does life invariably end up in a pigsty, or do some people seem to do rather well when they do their own thing?

3. Do you think that the son enjoyed his wild fling and got a lot out of his hedonistic lifestyle? Many seem to expect young people to rebel and get swept away into a hedonistic kind of lifestyle. What can result from even a few years of this kind of rebellion?

4. When we see our kids or our loved ones 'in the pigsty', how does it feel? What can we do to reach them? Is there a time to just 'sit and pray'? How should we react if we are rejected?

5. If we bring memories, situations or experiences which resulted from our own 'rebellion' to the Lord can He 'heal them'? Is it important to do this? If so ... why?

Open Our Eyes

When we choose to disobey the Lord's plans for our lives we take a perilous path. The prodigal son chose a life of wild parties, prostitutes and fun … but it didn't last for long. The experience was damaging to him and to those he loved.

This kind of lifestyle often leads to a kind of 'inner chaos'. Oscar Wilde tried to describe his own feelings and the effect of this fallenness on him, and those around him. He wrote …

> The gods had given me almost everything. But I let myself be lured into long spells of senseless and sensual ease … Tired of being on the heights, I deliberately went to the depths in search of new sensation. What the paradox was to me in the sphere of thought, perversity became to me in the sphere of passion. I grew careless of the lives of others. I took pleasure where it pleased me, and passed on. I forgot that every little action of the common day makes or unmakes character, and that therefore what one has done in the secret chamber, one has some day to cry aloud from the house-top. I ceased to be lord over myself. I was no longer the captain of my soul, and did not know it. I allowed pleasure to dominate me. I ended in horrible disgrace. (Quoted from Oscar Wilde by William Barclay, in *The Letters to the Galatians and Ephesians*, Philadelphia, Westminster, 1976, p.100.)

Yet, even in this kind of 'inner chaos' God reaches out to us and offers us His gift of 'amazing grace'. Even here, 'in the pigsty' He offers us a 'new beginning' and the opportunity to take the first step on the road back home.

WEEK 3

The Long Road Home

Opening Icebreaker

Describe a journey that you've been on. Maybe a journey to visit a far overseas destination ... or a journey to a favourite holiday destination in the UK.

What do you remember most about the journey? Do we sometimes treat journeys as 'dead time' rather than as rich experiences in themselves?

Get Involved ...

- Do you ever see life as a journey?

- What kind of journey has your life been, and where are you on this journey right now?

- Do you think that sometimes we're so preoccupied with the past or the future that we miss enjoying each stage of our journey day by day?

Bible Reading

The Prodigal Son: Luke 15:17–20

Dig Deeper

1. What does it mean 'he came to his senses'? What was going on in his mind?
2. Why did he compare his situation to the hired men rather than to his older brother?
3. Do you feel at all sorry for the prodigal?
4. How would his father have felt if he'd known his son was 'in the pigsty'?

Insight Readings

Our three insight readings all explore aspects of our relationship with God. They each help us to understand just how crucial this rich relationship is to normal Christian living. Divide into three or more groups to explore these biblical insights.

John 15:1–16
What does Jesus' teaching say about the nature of our

relationship with Him?

John 16:5–16
What does Jesus' teaching tell us about the work of the Holy Spirit in our relationship with Him?

Romans 8:1–17
What does Paul in Romans tell us about the work of the Holy Spirit in our 'journey of salvation'?

Insight Comment

The Holy Spirit is at work in each stage of the journey of salvation.

The grace of God was at work in the son even when he was in the pigsty. It was at work in his thinking about life back home. It was at work in the small but significant decisions which led to him turning towards home. It was at work on the journey home, and it was evident when his father raced to meet him.

Sometimes we think that God doesn't care about non-Christians, or that He isn't at work in their lives. Nothing could be further from the truth!

In Romans 8, Paul makes it clear that the Holy Spirit is active in the ongoing development of our relationship with God. A quick review of Romans 8 shows that through Him …

• We are set free from the law of sin and death. Without the help of the Holy Spirit we are powerless to do anything outside of our sinful nature (vv.1–4).

• Our minds begin to tune in to what God wants. Through the activity of the Holy Spirit we are able to overcome the power of sin with all its deadly effects (v.5).

- We discover the daily life which God wants us to enjoy. Only by the Spirit of God can we have victory over temptation and evil in our lives. In fact, without the Holy Spirit we cannot even belong to Christ (vv.6–9).

- We receive the guarantee of eternal life, and know that the day will come when we will rise to live with Christ forever. But eternal life is not just for the future; it is an experience that begins when we follow Christ (vv.10–11).

- We know how to live and what to do. The Spirit bears witness to the fact that we are God's children and gives us the confidence to approach Him as 'Abba, Father' (vv.12–17).

Prayers of Intercession

We pause to pray for those who may be known to us who as yet have not responded, but who God knows, loves and is – even now – speaking to! We pray for the work of the Holy Spirit in their lives.

The Long Road Home

WEEK THREE

Discussion Starters

1. When people move into Christian discipleship after a time of rebellion and disobedience, what support do they need? When Christians have fallen away and want to return, should they be disciplined first?

2. Are there different levels of intimacy with God? Do we become satisfied too soon? How can we strive to 'move out of the shallows' and to be immersed in His power and presence?

3. How can we best witness to and care for those who are away from the Father and out of His will? How can the Holy Spirit use us to influence the direction of their journey?

4. How have you experienced God in your own life? Were you aware of Him before you became a Christian, and do you think He was active in your life?

5. Does God's work of grace in our lives end the day we become believers? If not, what else is to be done? How can we co-operate and be sensitive to His ongoing plans for our lives?

25

Open Our Eyes

Too much evangelism is done in the power of human personality and creativity, and not enough is done in the power of God. Too much evangelism ends up weak and ineffectual because it has failed to draw on the resources of the Holy Spirit. Yet it is His ministry we are a part of; it is His task to convict men and women of sin and to begin the process of conversion. The part we play simply involves enabling people to discover His renewing and transforming power in their lives.

Evangelism is no more than us coming into partnership with the Holy Spirit as He continues to do what He is already doing in people's lives. If we try to do evangelism without Him, we will find it impossible.

We need the Spirit's power if we are to communicate with those who are blinded by the 'god of this age'. Even more, we need His discernment and authority if we are to break down spiritual strongholds so that men and women can be set free:

> For though we live in the world, we do not wage war as the world does. The weapons we fight with are not the weapons of the world. On the contrary, they have divine power to demolish strongholds.
> (2 Cor. 10:4)

How ludicrous it is that we should even think of engaging in evangelism without working with the creative power of God! How strange that we should try to evangelise without the Spirit whose work it really is! How ridiculous that we should try to evangelise without using the driving force He has given specifically for the task! The grace of God is working throughout the process of conversion, and He is often active in people's lives in beautiful and subtle ways beyond our understanding. We must pray for discernment to see what God is doing in their journey of life, and learn to work in tune with God's Spirit.

WEEK 4

A Robe and a Ring

Opening Icebreaker

Describe some of the times when you've had to 'dress up' in your finest! Was it for a wedding, a ball or a royal occasion? What did you wear, and how did it make you feel?

Get Involved ...

• Have you ever heard about or known someone who did something so generous that it seemed a bit excessive?

• What is generosity, and what makes us generous?

Bible Reading

The Prodigal Son: Luke 15:22–24

Dig Deeper

1. How do you think the servants felt when the father told them to bring these things?
2. Why was the father in such a hurry?
3. Why the best robe?
4. Why shouldn't the son robe himself?
5. Why was the ring important?
6. What state would his feet have been in?
7. Why was footwear so significant in that culture?
8. How do you think that the son felt about these gifts?
9. Why was the father so generous?
10. Why should this son have the best of everything?

Insight Readings

Our three sets of insight readings all explore aspects of the generosity of God, and help us to understand how He wants to give of His very best for us. His generosity is unstinting, lavish and without reserve!

Isaiah 61:10; Zechariah 3:1–5; Revelation 7:9
What do these passages tell us about the symbolism of clothes in the father's gift of a robe?

Genesis 41:41–43; Esther 3:9–11
What do these passages tell us about the symbolism of the father's gift of a ring?

1 Samuel 2:6–9; John 13:5; Romans 16:20
What do these passages tell us about the symbolism of the father's care for his son's feet?

Insight Comment

Jesus loved the world with a depth of compassion we can't begin to understand. His leap from heaven to earth was made at enormous personal cost and led to painful experiences of rejection.

He was rejected by the people He grew up with, who had known Him all his life. Going back to Nazareth, back to the carpenter's shop, back to His mother and brothers, and the small close-knit community in which He'd been reared, He might have expected a hero's welcome. Maybe they'd put the flags out for the small-town boy made good. Not a bit of it! Instead, He met only resistance and murderous hostility.

He was snubbed by the religious elite. When Simon, a Pharisee, invited Jesus to dinner, he didn't invite Him to honour Him, hear Him or affirm Him. He offered Him none of the marks of hospitality that a Jewish host of the time would have offered his guests – there was no kiss of welcome, no ceremonial washing bowl, no neatly folded towel. Instead, Jesus met with cynicism and mockery. It seems that Simon invited Jesus to humiliate Him!

He was rejected by His fellow countrymen. I remember one evening, at sunset, standing on the Mount of Olives, looking down over Jerusalem. It brought alive for me that moment when Jesus looked over that same city and wept:

'O Jerusalem, Jerusalem, you who kill the prophets and stone those sent to you, how often I have longed to gather your children together, as a hen gathers her chicks under her wings, but you were not willing.' (Luke 13:34)

Jesus had an aching burden for the people of that great city. He knew their needs and wanted to embrace them with His love. These were not empty sentiments but the expression of the One who lived entirely for others and who was feeling deep within Himself the pain of their rejection of Him.

And finally, He was betrayed and abandoned by His closest friends, the ones whom He might have expected to stick by Him through any danger. But when the guards came to arrest Him in Gethsemane, they were led there by one of His own disciples and all the others fled in terror, leaving Him to face His enemies alone.

Over and over again, the story of Jesus is a story of rejection. He was born in a borrowed stable and buried in a borrowed tomb, and between the two He knew what it was to walk a lonely road. It's little wonder, then, that He was often the friend of the rejected, and shrank from no one.

So it is all the more wonderful that the One who was rejected is the One who welcomes and accepts us! Just as He cared for crooks like Zacchaeus, those of dubious morality like the woman of Samaria, and outcasts like the ten lepers, He comes alongside us when we feel rejected and marginalised today.

His love speaks powerfully to anyone who has tasted abandonment and loneliness. His life teaches that through Him we can find acceptance, healing and adoption into the family of God.

The One who was rejected runs to greet us, and provides a robe for our back, a ring for our finger and shoes for our feet. We may come in fear of yet more rejection when we come to the Lord … but no, He races to embrace us!

Discussion Starters

1. The word which the father speaks – 'Quick' – reminds us of the urgency of the gospel, and the Father's eagerness to usher in the 'new kingdom'. Why is the Christian message so urgent?

2. The son was transformed from 'tatters to riches' in a matter of minutes. In which ways do we become rich when we find Christ? Can there be a financial blessing as well?

3. Bare feet are often a symbol of slavery. How does Christian faith 'set us free'?

4. The signet ring in the time of Jesus was rich in significance! It symbolised power and authority. What kind of power and authority does God's kingdom give to us, and how should we use it?

5. Do you find it hard to be generous? Why is generosity important to a Christian lifestyle? Why does God love a generous giver?

Open Our Eyes

Jesus ushered in the kingdom of God by demonstrating
His authority over the supernatural world, and over
disease and death. He cast out demons, healed those who
were sick, made the blind see, the lame walk and the
deaf hear. He commanded nature's obedience by stilling
the storm and walking on water. He raised people from
the dead to new life. Likewise, the apostles were known
not only for their preaching and good works, but also for
their ability to perform miracles and thus demonstrate that
the power of God really works.

In Philip's ministry, we see this clearly illustrated (see
Acts 8:4–8). When the crowds heard Philip and saw the
miraculous signs he did, they all paid close attention
to what he said. When we become Christians the Lord
gives us a 'ring of authority', and we are to use the gifts
of the Spirit to change the world and to demonstrate His
kingdom.

Many of us need to recognise God's sovereign ability to
break into our world with signs, wonders and miracles.
John Wimber once commented, 'In pragmatic evangelism
we say something and God acts, but in power evangelism
God says something and we act.' In this kind of witness,
demonstration and proclamation go hand in hand.

In my travels around the world I have come across many
situations in which power evangelism has been mightily
used by God – incredible healings, the miraculous arrival
of rain or the dramatic conversion of violent criminals.
I have not seen much power evangelism at work in the
United Kingdom, and have sometimes wondered what
kind of effect miraculous events would have in such a
cynical secularised culture as the one in which we live
today. Each of us should be eager to wear the ring of
authority, which is such an important part of being a
Christian.

WEEK 5

Dead and Alive

Opening Icebreaker

Describe a 'best friend' or a 'special friend' from your youth or childhood.

What are the ingredients of a great relationship?

Get Involved ...

- Why do some relationships grow richer and more meaningful over the years while others wither and die?

- Is being able to say 'sorry' a crucial part of long-lasting relationships?

Bible Reading

The Prodigal Son: Luke 15:19–24

Dig Deeper

1. Why was the son so sure that his father would reject him?
2. How did the son measure his 'self-worth'?
3. What difference is there in the relationship between a man and his servant and a man and his son?
4. Why did the father run to the son and not vice versa?
5. What physical contact was there between the father and his son? Was this significant?
6. What do you think the son smelt like?
7. Why do you think that the father was filled with compassion when he saw his son?
8. Why do you think that the father had viewed his son as 'dead' and 'lost'?
9. How do you think that their relationship changed through this experience?
10. Can you ever be 'worthy' of a relationship?

Insight Readings

Our three groups of insight readings all explore aspects of the 'character' of God, and help us to understand just how full of grace He really is! Divide into three or more groups to explore these biblical insights.

Luke 14:34–35; Psalm 17:8; 36:7; Malachi 4:2
What do these phrases tell us about the character of God?

Luke 11:9–13; Romans 8:15, 23; 9:4; Galatians 4:5
What do these phrases tell us about the fatherhood of God?

2 Samuel 12:7–14; John 8:3–11; Acts 9:1–6
What do these stories tell us about the forgiveness of God?

Insight Comment

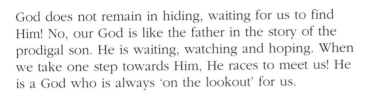

God does not remain in hiding, waiting for us to find Him! No, our God is like the father in the story of the prodigal son. He is waiting, watching and hoping. When we take one step towards Him, He races to meet us! He is a God who is always 'on the lookout' for us.

One Sunday the ex-politician Jonathan Aitken wrote an open letter in a Sunday newspaper to the novelist Jeffrey Archer, who had just begun his prison sentence. Jonathan, who had been a member of John Major's cabinet before he 'fell from grace' and ended up in prison himself, has become a born-again Christian.

In his open letter he reminded the famous peer, Lord Archer, of the grace of God that he had discovered in his own life and assured him that if he took one step towards God, the Father would race to embrace him!

This love, forgiveness and acceptance is at the very heart of our heavenly Father. It has nothing to do with how we value ourselves, or whether we are worthy of being rescued. We are the subjects of a Father's love which keeps on loving! If we have not grasped the enormity of this grace, how can we begin to live a new life?

The Swiss theologian Karl Barth was once asked what he thought was the most profound concept in Christianity. He replied, 'Jesus loves me, this I know, for the Bible tells me so.' Sometimes we can make Christianity so complicated that we forget the most profound truth of all! The Father is able to redeem us when we allow Him to take over our lives, and to push out sin's domination and ownership. He redeems us from slavery to our past, our failure, our sinfulness and our selfishness, and sets us free.

The work of redemption isn't all one way. It demands a first step from us, and a willingness to cast ourselves entirely upon His mercy.

It's a partnership between our Redeemer and ourselves. It's allowing Him to take the misshapen clay of our lives and letting Him mould it into something new, something better, something beautiful. It's more than we could ever deserve, far more than we can ever be worthy of … it's the most outrageous grace of all.

When we are forgiven, we need to pass on this grace to others. As Jesus taught us, 'Forgive us our trepasses as we forgive those who trespass against us.'

Discussion Starters

1. Do you believe that God sits and waits for us, or that, when we stray, He is actively searching for us? Have you ever been aware that He was looking for you?

2. Can we judge ourselves too harshly and value ourselves too cheaply or of no value? If we get into this way of thinking, how can it affect our faith, our relationships and our lifestyle?

3. What are the characteristics of a good father? What difference does a good father make to the quality of his children's lives? How should the quality of the Father's life change our perspective?

4. Have you ever met anyone who viewed themselves so critically and valued themselves so cheaply that they were unable to accept just how much God loves them? How can we help people who feel like this?

5. Do some Christians live their lives more like 'hired workers' than sons and daughters of the Father? If so, why? What do they need to learn?

Open Our Eyes

Stephen Oake, a 40-year-old Special Branch officer, was murdered in a Manchester flat. The killer? A terrorist who was the chemist behind the production of ricin poison in North London. The Greater Manchester Police team, backed by two immigration officers, had been told by MI5 that the 23-year-old asylum seeker would be in the flat in Crumpsall Lane, North Manchester. When they broke down the door, they were confronted by three men, not one, as they had expected.

When one of the men was recognised, and his details sent to Scotland Yard, the order came to seal the flat off amid fears that the chemist had set up another poison factory. At this point the man was asked to wear a forensic suit and, according to police, 'went berserk'. In the ensuing struggle, Detective Constable Stephen Oake was fatally stabbed in the chest.

The anguish and agony which this brief incident represented is quite incalculable. For those of us in the Christian community the full tragedy of it all was brought home when we heard that Stephen Oake was a committed Christian, a housegroup leader at Poynton Baptist Church, and a leader of the Manchester Branch of the Christian Police Association.

In the main evening news, however, in a brief 30-second statement, his father, Robin Oake – the former Chief Constable of the Isle of Man – demonstrated grace, when he summed up the power of the Christian gospel in a sentence. At a time when people would have expected a violent outburst about judgment and retribution, they heard about love. He said: 'I am praying for the perpetrator of this killing and seeking God's forgiveness for him – praying also that he may now seek God himself and find peace and forgiveness with Him.'

WEEK 6

Party Time

Opening Icebreaker

What was the most memorable party you ever went to?

What are the ingredients of a great party?

Get Involved ...

• Why are parties important?

• What kind of things should we celebrate?

• Do you think that Christians have enough parties?

Bible Reading

The Prodigal Son: Luke 15:23–27

Dig Deeper

1. What kind of things did they do at the father's party?
2. What do the words 'make merry' imply?
3. Why was it fitting to hold a party?
4. Why did Jesus tell the parables in Luke 15 in the first place?
5. What did He hope to teach the Pharisees and scribes through these stories?
6. Compare the emotions felt by the shepherd (v.6), the woman (v.9), and the father (v.24).
7. Why is there joy in heaven? (v.7).
8. What do the three stories in Luke 15 tell us about the character of God? Why does God rejoice?
9. What do these stories tell us about heaven?
10. The Pharisees were always suggesting that Jesus was mixing with the wrong people! Why did Jesus do that, and what does it tell us about grace?

Insight Readings

Our four insight readings explore the Bible teaching about banquets. Time and again we see that when there is a party in the kingdom of God it isn't a 'finger buffet' or cheap-skate barbecue. It's a full-blown banquet!

As a whole group read Revelation 19:6–9. What kind of celebration was this? Who was it for? Why a 'wedding party'?

In small groups read one of the following passages, and try to 'get into' the thinking of the main characters.

Luke 14:12–24
What does the guest list in these parables tell us about God's grace?

Luke 13:22–30
Who will get in and who won't get in, and what does this tell us about God's grace?

Luke 15:1–10
What do these two parables teach about God's reasons for a party?

Insight Comment

The father in the prodigal story really wanted to have a great celebration when his son came home. It was a celebration to express his ecstatic joy and indescribable happiness at the arrival of his son 'who was dead, but who is alive!'

Anyone who has lost a child – even for half an hour – can relate to the kind of ecstasy you feel when the child is found. Anyone who has lived through a period of painful 'teenage rebellion' knows how great it feels when it's over. This father was so happy to have his son back!

The joy which the father felt reveals just how much he loved his son, and just how much he missed him. The story of the prodigal son reveals much about the character of God. He is a God who loves, who reaches out to the lost and who rejoices when they are found!

We worship a God who longs for relationship, a God who longs to forgive, a God who longs to restore, and a God who knows how to have a great party!

The different parables about lostness and about invitations to parties that we find in Luke 15 give us a clear and poignant insight into the very character of God!

If we were to grasp the significance of these stories we

might get an insight into the extravagant love of God for each of us. God rejoices about the return of just one lost person! This is a God who not only loves the nations, but who also loves and values individuals. At the heart of God there is a desire for intimacy with each of us, and a longing for relationship with each of us.

Do I really understand just how much God loves me, just how important I am to Him, and just how much He longs to live in close harmony with me every day of my life?

In all of the 'lost' parables, the joy of recovering the lost sheep, the lost coin and the lost son is always a joy to be shared. God doesn't keep this joy to Himself. He shares it and allows others to become an integral part of it.

The God we worship is a God of community, a God of relationship, a God who celebrates with the angels, a God who encourages us all to invite everyone to share in the joy of what His grace is about!

Another aspect of God's character revealed by these parables is that God chooses joy over remorse and recrimination. Some fathers would have seen the return of the son as a reason for a showdown or a row. But in this instance the father sees it as the reason for a good party. He chooses to forgive, to accept, to love, and to celebrate. This gives us an important insight into the character of God – a character infused with grace. A God who chooses to forgive!

Discussion Starters

1. The father was extravagant in organising such a great party. Is God's grace extravagant, over-the-top and unwarranted? If we really understood just how extravagant God's grace is, how would we live?

2. Did you ever know the joy of seeing someone far away from God be restored in relationship to Him? What was it like? How did it feel? What did it tell you about God? Have you ever lived without a sense of relationship with God? How did it feel? What was it like?

3. What is joy? Is it different from happiness?

4. Do you have any idea what heaven will be like? Is the image of a banquet a help or a hindrance to you? How do you think we will celebrate in heaven?

5. Do you think that we've squeezed out emotion and sanitised our feelings too often in church life? What should we rejoice about? Have you ever known a spontaneously joyful Christian?

Open Our Eyes

Charles Wesley was a regular prison visitor to Newgate
Jail in London. While visiting one prisoner who was
sick with fever and condemned to be hanged, Charles
explained the good news of the cross to him.

> I told him of one who came down from heaven to
> save lost sinners, and him in particular. I described
> the sufferings of the Son of God, His sufferings,
> agony and death. He listened with all the signs
> of eager astonishment; the tears trickled down his
> cheeks while he cried 'What? Was it for me? Did God
> suffer all this for so poor a creature as me?' (*Charles
> Wesley's Journal*, 17 July 1771.)

On the morning of the hanging Charles went to meet the
'death cart' as it drove towards the gallows. There was a
large crowd there, and they were taunting the prisoners.
When the prisoner saw Charles 'he smiled with the most
composed, delightful countenance I ever saw.' (*Charles
Wesley's Journal*, 19 July 1771.) Charles mounted the
death cart, and he and all the prisoners sang together:

> Behold the Saviour of mankind
> Nail'd to the shameful tree!
> How vast the love that Him inclined
> To bleed and die for thee!
> 'Tis done! The precious ransom's paid;
> 'Receive My Soul', He cries;
> See where He bows His sacred head!
> He bows His head, and dies!
> A guilty, weak and helpless worm,
> Into Thy hands I fall;
> Be Thou my life, my righteousness,
> My Jesus and my all.

'When the cart drew off,' wrote Charles, 'not one struggled
for life. We left them going to meet their Lord.'

WEEK 7

Sour Grapes

Opening Icebreaker

In Rembrandt's famous painting *The Return of the Prodigal Son* the canvas is dominated by the figure of the older son.

- If you were painting the older son how would you imagine him, and how would you portray him?

- If you are an 'arty' kind of group why not have a go at drawing or painting what you think he might have looked like and how he would have dressed?

Get Involved ...

- Some scholars see the older son as an illustration of how the religious people in Israel responded to Jesus compared to non-religious Jews. Why?

- Do you think Jesus told the story with this in mind?

Bible Reading

The Prodigal Son: Luke 15:25–32

Dig Deeper

1. What do you think the older son was doing when his brother returned?
2. What effect did the music and dancing have on him?
3. How do you think he felt when the servant told him 'your brother has come'?
4. Why did the older brother 'refuse to go in'?
5. What do you think his father said to him?
6. What does the phrase 'slaving for you' tell us about his attitude towards his father?
7. Why had the father never even given him a goat?
8. Do you think the older son was bitter?
9. Why was the father's reply so poignant and powerful?
10. Do you feel any sympathy for the older son?

Insight Readings

Our three insight readings all explore aspects of the meaning of the story about the older son.

Jeremiah 31:10–20
What does this passage tell us about God's love for the scattered people of Israel?

Luke 18:9–14
What does this passage tell us about the way that people can shut themselves out of God's grace?

Matthew 20:1–16
What does this passage tell us about the grace of God … and how it turns the value systems of the world upside down?

Insight Comment

Mercy is the hallmark of the kingdom of God. Mercy is the characteristic of our heavenly Father, and mercy must be a core part of those who really belong to His kingdom. Mercy is the guarantee of human authenticity. Mercy is the sign of the living presence of God. Jesus taught: 'Blessed are the merciful, for they will be shown mercy.'

John outrightly condemned those who queued up on the riverbank to be baptised but whose lives did not measure up to the high standard of God's calling. He compared the religious hypocrites of his day to a 'brood of vipers', and was sarcastic about their claims to God's special favour just because they were the descendants of Abraham. (God can make more children of Abraham out of a pile of stones!)

John's ministry was a preparation for the arrival of Jesus. And he believed that the best way of preparing the people for the coming Messiah was by calling them to repentance and personal preparation.

No matter how uncomfortable we may find it, there is no escaping the fact that the teaching of Jesus is littered with powerful images of judgment, and He judges those who show no mercy with the harshest condemnation. His whole ministry was full of warnings to us that one day we must face Him as our Judge, and that our lack of mercy for others would put us among the goats rather than the sheep!

In the parable of the servant who owed the king ten thousand talents we learn that the king is merciful and forgives him the debt. But later, the same servant refused to forgive someone who owed him a measly one hundred denarii. As a result the king recalled him, and handed him over to the jailers to be held until he should repay his huge loan in full (Matt. 18:21–35).

In the parable of the sheep and goats, the peoples of the world are divided into two groups. Those who have ministered to the stranger in his hunger, thirst, loneliness, deprivation, sickness and imprisonment are led to one side, and those who refused to offer help and service to the other. Those who have failed in their duty 'will go to eternal punishment' (Matt. 25:31–46).

The story of the older son is a powerful and poignant reminder that we must be careful lest, in our religious fervour, we forget the grace of God, and do not pass it on to others. If we do not show mercy we exclude ourselves from the love and acceptance that He offers. God's judgment rests on those who don't respond to His grace, or offer grace to others.

Discussion Starters

1. How do you think the older son felt when his brother left the party? Why was the older brother so hard and uncompromising? What emotions were driving him?

2. The older son was full of anger, resentment and jealousy. How do these powerful emotions creep into our lives, even when we claim to follow Christ? What kinds of things can trigger such destructive behaviour?

3. The younger son left the house at the beginning of the story, and the older son left at the end. What happens when we 'leave the house' and distance ourselves from our heavenly Father?

4. Do you think the older son felt that he'd never really been properly valued, rewarded and affirmed? Could that possibly have been his fault? How?

5. What other stories and parables remind us that the Pharisees were rather like the older son? How can we, in the Church today, hold similar attitudes? Why are they so negative?

Open Our Eyes

No one ever told me about the judgment. In my denomination, judgment was an unspoken word, a biblical principle long buried by a ton of liberal books. But as the years have gone by I've become more and more aware of the impending judgment on my life, ministry and work.

Again and again across the years of my discipleship I've gradually become more aware of God's bottom line. For, indisputably, He has one. God has His own ways of measuring our success or failure. And I suspect that His 'league tables' are rather different from our own!

In my more reflective moments I can sense Him measuring my life. My plans might seem exciting to me, but they're useless unless they're given His nod of approval. My performance might seem outstanding to me, but it's hollow if my motives are wrong. My management might seem tightly efficient to me, but it's flawed if it isn't ultimately fully accountable to Him.

So, if I want to meet God's bottom line, I find that I must proceed with caution. I must regularly place my 'doing' in accountability to His 'being'. God's bottom line isn't about profit and loss; it's about right and wrong, love and hate, good and bad, truth and falsehood, integrity and double-dealing. God's bottom line isn't measured by success … it's about obedience, and faithfulness, and living a life given over to Him.

It's only His wisdom that can help me avoid evil, guard my soul, live humbly, trust Him, discern right, speak intelligently, and recognise that there's more to life than worldly success.

Leader's Notes

Week 1: The Hard Goodbye

Aim of the Session
The aim of this study is to communicate something about God's gift of 'free will', and to begin to grasp just how wonderful this gift is ... and how much it is a mark of 'God's grace toward us'.

Prayers of Thanksgiving
A short 'open time' of prayer thanking God for the gift of free will, and His undeserved love offered to us.

Prayers of Repentance
Either read a prayer of repentance or invite group members to lead the whole group in a time of repentance for those times in which we have rejected God's way and gone our own.

Prayer Focus - to end the session
Pray for families that are hurting, where home is a battlefield and relationships are fraught. Pray especially for parents who have had to 'let go' of their kids and watch them make big mistakes.

Notes
The Icebreaker should begin to open up lots of discussion about happy and sad goodbyes. Start the ball rolling with personal examples: maybe saying goodbye to a child at the schoolyard gate on the first day or taking a student to university for the first time! Try to get into that powerful mix of emotions we feel when we say goodbye. Try to begin to unpack these emotions as felt by the father and the son in the prodigal story.

The role play is optional, but if you can get someone to verbalise the emotions the son felt as he said goodbye to his dad it could help the group to 'get into' the story.

The 'Dig Deeper' questions are designed to help people to understand the passage. They are not intended to be the source of in-depth discussion!

The three Bible readings and associated questions give the group the opportunity to look at other occasions in which God gave people a choice. You may not have time for all three. Personally I find the relationship between Jesus and Judas the most moving and poignant.

There are three suggested spaces for prayer during the evening: the first a time of thanksgiving, the second of repentance and the third of intercession. You may choose to merge these at the end.

The five questions in the 'Discussion Starters' section are, for me, the most important aspect of the evening, and in particular questions 4 and 5. I hope that at least 20 minutes will be left for this section. Things discussed and shared are much more readily learnt than those things we just listen to!

Week 2: In the Pigsty

Aim of the Session

Our theme this week is about the resilience of God's grace, and how it doesn't let go of us even in our greatest rebellion.

Prayers of Thanksgiving

A short 'open time' of prayer thanking God for His gift of grace. We ask the Lord to give us a depth of compassion for those who are 'in the pigsty'. We ask Him to help us to judge less … and to love more!

Prayers of Healing

We bring in silence those memories of our own rebellion, or rejection of God's way. We ask Him to cover us with 'fresh grace', and to help us to move on. We remember to leave our 'old life' buried with Christ forever.

Prayer Focus – to end the session

Pray for 'broken families' and for children who are, as yet, still far away from home. Ask God's protection over them, and pray that they may yet discover the grace which reaches out to them.

Notes

Have some fun talking about your life at work … and the worst jobs you've ever had to do. If there aren't many stories in the group, chat about jobs you'd hate to do! Sewer maintenance, for example?

It's important to spend a few minutes chatting about pigsties. The prodigal in the pigsty is an important illustration of where a life of sin can lead! The 'Dig Deeper' questions are designed to get people relating to this concept.

This week we use three biblical examples – Jonah, the people of Israel and Thomas – to illustrate how the Lord still 'hangs on to us' even when we're not following or trusting Him. There are many other biblical examples; see if you can get the group to suggest others.

In the prayers of thanksgiving, do ask the Lord for gifts of sensitivity, understanding and compassion in caring for those who are 'in the pigsty'. So often Christians can be proud and judgmental, when none of us are any more than 'sinners saved by grace'.

The discussion questions begin to open up a new subject area. Just as we need to understand God's grace as it is available to others, we need to know this grace ourselves.

Some members of the group may have unconfessed sin relating to times of rebellion in their own lives. Others may need to bring memories and experiences back to the cross to be dealt with so that they can be healed and move on.

Obviously these are very sensitive areas, and the members of the group should not be pushed to do these things until they feel that they are ready.

The final prayer time can be quite emotional, particularly if there are divorcees, members of broken families or single parents present. Nevertheless, this could be an important time of ministry to them and of prayer for the 'prodigals' associated with the group. Make sure that this end prayer time is not rushed. A cup of tea would probably be very helpful when it's over!

Week 3: The Long Road Home

Aim of the Session

The important aspect of this study is that we are all on a journey 'home', like the prodigal son. That journey only ends when we have a personal audience with the King of kings ourselves.

Prayers of Repentance

The younger son returned home in emptiness, humiliation and defeat. Are there things that we need to bring before God, to receive His forgiveness for, and to move back into renewed fellowship with Him?

It might be appropriate for this to be a time of silent prayer, perhaps with music.

Prayer Focus - to end the session

We pray for those who are still 'far off' and for the Holy Spirit's influence upon them.

Notes

Throughout life's journey God loves us and cares for us, and even when we are 'far away' the Holy Spirit is active in our lives.

In evangelism we need to recognise that God is at work in those we are witnessing to; even if they don't know it!

These Christian insights are important if we are to understand our journey, and the journey of those all around us.

Week 4: A Robe and a Ring

Aim of the Session
To grasp the urgency of the kingdom of God and to appreciate the extravagance of God's love.

Prayers of Thanksgiving
Thank the Lord for the many gifts that He has showered upon us.

Prayers of Petition
Ask the Lord to melt our hearts, to give us a deeper sense of compassion, and to help us to be more spontaneously generous and loving in all that we do.

Prayer Focus – to end the session
Ask God to help us not only to know His grace, but to pass it on to others in all our relationships.

Notes
There are four important aspects of teaching in this study. The first is to encourage the group to begin to grasp the urgency of the kingdom of God; the second is to appreciate the extravagance of God's love; third, to grasp the importance of Christian generosity; and finally to understand the authority invested in us as members of God's kingdom.

Don't feel that you have to cover them all ... but undoubtedly two or three aspects of the teaching will be specially relevant for your group!

I was deeply challenged by the testimony of a newly retired secondary school headmaster of a large school in London. He confessed to me that he really discovered that prayer works only towards the end of his teaching career. He had become bored and fed up with a form of Christianity which seemed to lack credibility and power, so he started to 'put God to the test'.

He told me of incident after incident during the stressful years of leading a large school community, in which he dared to pray for miracles and told his staff and students that he was doing so. It was little wonder, therefore, that, when his prayers began to be answered in the lives of individuals and of the whole community, people began to listen to him. They became hungry to know more about a 'faith that works'.

Week 5 Dead and Alive

Aim of the Session
In this study we recognise that grace is at the heart of the character of God. He doesn't sit and wait for us to come home … He runs to meet us!

Prayers of Repentance
Bring to God those feelings of unworthiness, self-criticism, condemnation and guilt which are signs that we are living outside of grace. Bring to God those aspects of our lifestyle which make us more like hired workers than adopted children. Say sorry …

Prayers of Petition
Ask God to help us not only to know His grace, but to pass it on to others in all our relationships.

Prayer Focus – to end the session
Pray for those who feel unworthy of being loved, and who feel that they are unlovable. Pray for those who find it hard to love others.

Notes
There are two important focal points for this study. First, we must understand that knowing God's grace has implications for our lives, and on how we value ourselves.

The second main theme is that if we have received this grace ourselves, we must learn how to live it ... and discover how to pass it on!

Robin Oake's words were flashed around the world by CNN, Sky News and BBC News 24. A word from God in the midst of a chattering world. It ranked for me as one of those Jesus moments when the gospel stands above the news. The redemptive power of Jesus is beyond the politics of human revenge. The love of God is more powerful than the violent deeds of evildoers.

The awesome responsibility of knowing the grace of a forgiving father is that we have to live it, pass it on, and offer it to everyone we meet. Even those who wrong us deeply.

The work of Jesus in helping us to forgive is not an instantaneous, one-off act. It's a day on day, and year on year work of 'redemption'. If we let Him, He can take our scars, the wounds that go deep into our past. The hurts. The disappointments. The regrets. The dark shadows that haunt us down the years – and, quite literally, give us the grace to 'forgive those who trespass against us'.

God doesn't wave a magic wand over our lives and make it all better. No, redemption is a partnership between Jesus and ourselves. It's allowing Him to take the painful tragedies of life and letting Him mould them into something new. Something better. Something beautiful. Grace in action. It's one thing to receive the outrageous grace of Jesus. It's another to discover how to pass it on!

Week 6: Party Time

Aim of the Session

The amazing thing about God's grace is that it always applies to individuals. Although His grace is available to all, it is always about the transformation of individual men and women. That's why there is joy in heaven over 'one sinner who repents'. While we are often preoccupied with the numbers game, God is always interested in the individual. When just one life is transformed, there is reason enough for a party in heaven!

The story of the prodigal son raises an important question for each of us. If our Father demonstrates such a level of grace to each individual, how should this affect the way we live?

Prayers of Thanksgiving

A short 'open time' of prayer thanking God for who He is. We recognise His love, His generosity of grace, the richness of knowing Him and living with Him. We thank Him for our friends, those in our fellowship and for the joy of relationship, which is so much part of belonging to His family.

Prayers about Joy

We thank the Lord for what He has done in our lives, and in the lives of many others around us. We ask to know joy in our hearts and lives, and we seek to express it more spontaneously and readily. We ask God to give us the gift of joy!

Prayer Response – to end the session

Spend some moments in silence thinking about the love of the father in the parable. Remember how he decides to forgive, chooses to accept his son and opts to hold a party!

How should we then live? What kind of choices do we need to make if we are to live as the true children of our heavenly Father?

Notes

If we are to get into the theme it's important to enter into an understanding of parties, and how significant and meaningful they can be, so don't rush the Icebreaker or 'Get Involved...' section.

The three Insight Readings give the group an opportunity to explore other parables which teach about God's great invitation, to ask who will really be 'welcome' at the heavenly banquet, and to explore God's strange topsy-turvy set of priorities, which seem to make the people who are generally 'unwelcome' in society the guests of honour!

Do read the Revelation passage and explore there the concepts of 'banquet' and 'wedding feast'.

The Insight Comment and prayer time are designed to help the group reflect on the character of God, to begin to grasp just how central 'grace' is to our understanding of God, and to begin to verbalise it in prayers of thanksgiving. Some more cerebral and talkative groups may be ready to spend longer discussing the character of God than others.

All of the Discussion Starters are important if the group is to get the most out of this study, but most will be gained from the final question. If it's possible to brief some members of the group beforehand to share their story it might be helpful. Or you could invite a special guest for the evening to share their 'testimony'.

One thing's for sure, this teaching will really come to life if people start to talk about the transformational effect

which God's grace has had on their own life.
Feel free to miss out 'Open Our Eyes' if you have
contemporary stories of grace there in the group!

The final prayer time, Prayer Response, could be very
meaningful and important. In fact, it could trigger an
important discussion. So some groups might like to leave
space for this.

Charles Wesley knew what it was to rescue people from
the very pit of hell, and to set their feet on the road to
heaven.

This is what the story of the prodigal son is all about: the
joy of one person who finds forgiveness, cleansing and
a new beginning. And the day you find it is the day you
find heaven. What a great reason for a party!

But there is a sting in the tail. If our Father demonstrates
such grace, how should we live? On my radio programme
on Premier one morning Norman Kember, the Iraq
hostage, told me how he prayed for his kidnappers
– even while he was chained up for nearly four months.

If we worship a God of such grace we, too, must
exemplify that grace in the smallest and largest
experiences in life. For each is offered to us as an
opportunity to reflect to others what God has given to us.

Week 7: Sour Grapes

Aim of the Session
There is only one message behind this final study: that God's grace is available – but we *must* respond to it! This session provides a poignant challenge to all of us involved in church life to be careful lest we become judgmental, critical and proud. It's also a chance for those of us who have lived more like 'older brothers' to have the opportunity to have a new beginning like the prodigal son.

If you don't have a copy of Rembrant's painting, *The Return of the Prodigal Son,* maybe you could download one from the Internet for the group to see.

Prayers for Families
Pray for the families represented in the group, and especially for relationships between brothers and sisters. Pray against sibling rivalry!

Prayers of Petition
Ask the Lord to forgive us for the ways in which we have been resentful, lacked compassion, been judgmental of others, and walked away from the party!

Prayer Focus – to end the session
Those of us who have only ever thought of Jesus as Friend, Saviour, Comforter and Guide would do well to recognise that He is also our Judge. Today, and tomorrow; now, and in eternity. No one told me that one of the greatest priorities of my Christian life must be to make time for confession, for repentance, and for saying sorry.

Notes

God's bottom line will be revealed when I stand before Jesus at the end of time and hear Him ask, 'Well?' Sometimes, in my honest moments, I look towards my personal judgment day and I see little mercy in the person I've become. So many opportunities for kindness lost for good. So many chances to show love missed along the way. So many hurting people who remained ignored. Simple deeds that would have made lives different lie left undone.

No one warned me that out of all life's priorities I could overlook the most important of them all: to be merciful, compassionate, gracious and kind. To do the very things which would survive the fire of judgment day.

Perhaps, in the theological gamesmanship I've played, I've missed the potency of the simple truth that, while I was fixing my life on winning the world I had overlooked mercy and become more like the older brother than the prodigal son.

Make sure that there is ample time for the message about 'hardness of spirit' to get rooted in the conversation, and give sufficient opportunity for those present to dump those petty rivalries and bitter attitudes which can so easily sour our outlook. End with an opportunity for repentance.

Whether in these studies you have identified most with the younger son or with the older son, it's good to recognise that there is grace sufficient for you. In coming back to the Father's love from a life of rebellion or a life of spiritual pride, His arms are open wide and His grace as amazing as ever.

NATIONAL DISTRIBUTORS

UK: (and countries not listed below)
CWR, Waverley Abbey House, Waverley Lane, Farnham, Surrey GU9 8EP.
Tel: (01252) 784700 Outside UK (44) 1252 784700 Email: mail@cwr.org.uk

AUSTRALIA: KI Entertainment, Unit 21 317-321 Woodpark Road, Smithfield, New South Wales 2164.
Tel: 1 800 850 777 Fax: 02 9604 3699 Email: sales@kientertainment.com.au

CANADA: David C Cook Distribution Canada, PO Box 98, 55 Woodslee Avenue, Paris, Ontario N3L 3E5.
Tel: 1800 263 2664 Email: swansons@cook.ca

GHANA: Challenge Enterprises of Ghana, PO Box 5723, Accra.
Tel: (021) 222437/223249 Fax: (021) 226227 Email: ceg@africaonline.com.gh

HONG KONG: Cross Communications Ltd, 1/F, 562A Nathan Road, Kowloon.
Tel: 2780 1188 Fax: 2770 6229 Email: cross@crosshk.com

INDIA: Crystal Communications, 10-3-18/4/1, East Marredpalli, Secunderabad – 500026, Andhra Pradesh.
Tel/Fax: (040) 27737145 Email: crystal_edwj@rediffmail.com

KENYA: Keswick Books and Gifts Ltd, PO Box 10242-00400, Nairobi.
Tel: (254) 20 312639/3870125 Email: keswick@swiftkenya.com

MALAYSIA: Salvation Book Centre (M) Sdn Bhd, 23 Jalan SS 2/64, 47300 Petaling Jaya, Selangor.
Tel: (03) 78766411/78766797 Fax: (03) 78757066/78756360
Email: info@salvationbookcentre.com

Canaanland, No. 25 Jalan PJU 1A/41B, NZX Commercial Centre, Ara Jaya, 47301 Petaling Jaya, Selangor.
Tel: (03) 7885 0540/1/2 Fax: (03) 7885 0545 Email: info@canaanland.com.my

NEW ZEALAND: KI Entertainment, Unit 21 317-321 Woodpark Road, Smithfield, New South Wales 2164, Australia.
Tel: 0 800 850 777 Fax: +612 9604 3699 Email: sales@kientertainment.com.au

NIGERIA: FBFM, Helen Baugh House, 96 St Finbarr's College Road, Akoka, Lagos.
Tel: (01) 7747429/4700218/825775/827264 Email: fbfm@hyperia.com

PHILIPPINES: OMF Literature Inc, 776 Boni Avenue, Mandaluyong City.
Tel: (02) 531 2183 Fax: (02) 531 1960 Email: gloadlaon@omflit.com

SINGAPORE: Alby Commercial Enterprises Pte Ltd, 95 Kallang Avenue #04-00, AIS Industrial Building, 339420.
Tel: (65) 629 27238 Fax: (65) 629 27235 Email: marketing@alby.com.sg

SOUTH AFRICA: Struik Christian Books, 80 MacKenzie Street, PO Box 1144, Cape Town 8000.
Tel: (021) 462 4360 Fax: (021) 461 3612 Email: info@struikchristianmedia.co.za

SRI LANKA: Christombu Publications (Pvt) Ltd, Bartleet House, 65 Braybrooke Place, Colombo 2.
Tel: (9411) 2421073/2447665 Email: dhanad@bartleet.com

USA: David C Cook Distribution Canada, PO Box 98, 55 Woodslee Avenue, Paris, Ontario N3L 3E5, Canada. Tel: 1800 263 2664 Email: swansons@cook.ca

CWR is a Registered Charity - Number 294387
CWR is a Limited Company registered in England -
Registration Number 1990308

Day and Residential Courses

Counselling Training

Leadership Development

Biblical Study Courses

Regional Seminars

Ministry to Women

Daily Devotionals

Books and DVDs

Conference Centre

Trusted all Over the World

CWR HAS GAINED A WORLDWIDE reputation as a centre of excellence for Bible-based training and resources. From our headquarters at Waverley Abbey House, Farnham, England, we have been serving God's people for over 40 years with a vision to help apply God's Word to everyday life and relationships. The daily devotional *Every Day with Jesus* is read by nearly a million people in more than 150 countries, and our unique courses in biblical studies and pastoral care are respected all over the world. Waverley Abbey House provides a conference centre in a tranquil setting.

For free brochures on our seminars and courses, conference facilities, or a catalogue of CWR resources, please contact us at the following address.
CWR, Waverley Abbey House, Waverley Lane, Farnham, Surrey GU9 8EP, UK

Telephone: **+44 (0)1252 784700**
Email: mail@cwr.org.uk
Website: www.cwr.org.uk

CWR Applying God's Word
to everyday life and relationships

Dramatic new resources

2 Corinthians: Restoring harmony
by Christine Platt

Paul's message went against the grain of the culture in Corinth, and even his humility was in stark contrast to Greco-Roman culture. Be challenged and inspired to endure suffering, seek reconciliation, pursue holiness and much more as you look at this moving letter which reveals Paul's heart as much as his doctrine. This thought-provoking, seven-week study guide is great for individual or small-group use.
ISBN: 978-1-85345-551-3

Isaiah 40–66: Prophet of restoration
by John Houghton

God is a God of new beginnings, a God of second chances who takes no pleasure in punishment. However, profound lessons must be learned if the same errors are to be avoided in the future. Understand Isaiah's powerful message for each of us, that God is a holy God who cannot ignore sin, but One who also displays amazing grace and mercy, and who longs to enjoy restored relationship with us. These seven inspiring and challenging studies are perfect for individual or small-group use.
ISBN: 978-1-85345-550-6

Also available in the bestselling
Cover to Cover Bible Study Series

1 Corinthians
Growing a Spirit-filled church
ISBN: 978-1-85345-374-8

1 Timothy
Healthy churches – effective Christians
ISBN: 978-1-85345-291-8

23rd Psalm
The Lord is my shepherd
ISBN: 978-1-85345-449-3

2 Timothy and Titus
Vital Christianity
ISBN: 978-1-85345-338-0

Ecclesiastes
Hard questions and spiritual answers
ISBN: 978-1-85345-371-7

Ephesians
Claiming your inheritance
ISBN: 978-1-85345-229-1

Esther
For such a time as this
ISBN: 978-1-85345-511-7

Fruit of the Spirit
Growing more like Jesus
ISBN: 978-1-85345-375-5

Genesis 1–11
Foundations of reality
ISBN: 978-1-85345-404-2

God's Rescue Plan
Finding God's fingerprints on human histo
ISBN: 978-1-85345-294-9

Great Prayers of the Bible
Applying them to our lives today
ISBN: 978-1-85345-253-6

Hebrews
Jesus – simply the best
ISBN: 978-1-85345-337-3

Hosea
The love that never fails
ISBN: 978-1-85345-290-1

Isaiah 1–39
Prophet to the nations
ISBN: 978-1-85345-510-0

£3.99 each (plus p&p)
Price correct at time of printing

Cover to Cover Every Day

Gain deeper knowledge of the Bible

Each issue of these bimonthly daily Bible-reading notes gives you insightful commentary on a book of the Old and New Testaments with reflections on a psalm each weekend by Philip Greenslade.

Enjoy contributions from two well-known authors every two months, and over a five-year period you will be taken through the entire Bible.

ISSN: 1744-0114

Only £2.49 each (plus p&p)

£13.80 for annual UK subscription (6 issues)

£13.80 for annual email subscription

(available from www.cwr.org.uk/store)

MAY/JUN 2010
Esther
Matthew 1–7

Every Day

Esther
Mary Evans

Matthew 1–7
Philip Greenslade

WEEKEND REFLECTIONS ON THE USE OF PSALMS IN THE NEW TESTAMENT

BRINGING YOU DEEPER BIBLICAL UNDERSTANDING   CWR

Cover to Cover Complete

Read through the Bible chronologically

Take an exciting, year-long journey through the Bible, following events as they happened.

- See God's strategic plan of redemption unfold across the centuries
- Increase your confidence in the Bible as God's inspired message
- Come to know your heavenly Father in a deeper way

The full text of the flowing Holman Christian Standard Bible (HCSB) provides an exhilarating reading experience and is augmented by our beautiful:

- Illustrations
- Maps
- Charts
- Diagrams
- Timeline

And key Scripture verses and devotional thoughts make each day's reading more meaningful.

ISBN: 978-1-85345-433-2
Only £19.99 (plus p&p)

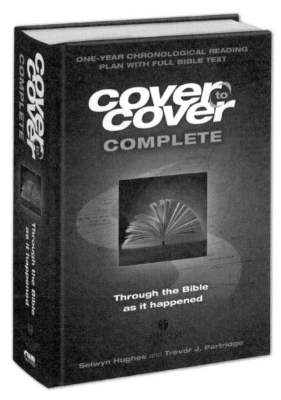